Audit. Review. Compila
What's the difference?

Illustrations using a football game,
buying a used car, and filling a bucket

Audit. Review. Compilation. What's the difference?

Illustrations using a football game, buying a used car, and filling a bucket

James L. Ulvog, CPA

RS

Riverstone Finance Press
Alta Loma, California

www.riverstonefinancepress.com

Audit. Review. Compilation. What's the difference?
Illustrations using a football game, buying a used car,
and filling a bucket

The text in this book is a compilation of posts previously published in the author's weblog, Nonprofit Update (nonprofitupdate.info). The posts have been edited from when they originally appeared.

This book is distributed with the understanding that the author and publisher are not rendering accounting or other professional services in this publication. If accounting advice or expert assistance is required, the services of a competent professional should be retained.

Published by:
Riverstone Finance Press
8780 19th St. #305
Alta Loma, CA 91701

riverstonefinancepress.com

Cover design by Caligraphics.   http://caligraphics.net

ISBN-13: 978-0-9774361-0-1

Contents

Introduction 1

'Preparing' financial statements - a new level of service 3

Football illustration 5

How you would check out a used car if you
    audited, reviewed, or compiled its condition? 7

A detailed explanation 11

Filling up a bucket with water 15

Levels of assurance 19

About the author

Other books by this author

Introduction

There are three main levels of services a CPA can provide your business or nonprofit organization. These are an audit, a review, and a compilation.

How are those different? This short book will help you understand the differences between those services.

Three different illustrations paint a picture of the differences. Additional comments provide more of a technical description.

This is a compilation of posts previously published on my blog, Nonprofit Update (nonprofitupdate.info). They have been revised from when they were originally published, yet with the goal of retaining the casual writing style of the blog.

We start with a new level of service that might be available from CPAs in the near future.

Audit. Review. Compilation.

'Preparing' financial statements - A new level of services -

You are probably aware of three levels of service a CPA can provide - audit, review, and compilation.

In October 2013, the people who set audit rules issued a proposal which creates a new level of service. This will be called preparation of financial statements.

Such service will not be subject to the same rules that govern compilations, reviews, or audits.

When the client organization and CPA agree to this approach, the accountant can issue a set of financial statements without any cover report from the accountant.

The accountant will not be obtaining any assurance on the financial statements and users should not infer any assurance.

The accountant doesn't have to do any work to verify any of the information is correct. Paragraph 3 of the exposure draft says an accountant

> "...is not required to verify the accuracy or completeness of the information provided by management or otherwise gather evidence to express an opinion or a conclusion on the financial statements or otherwise report on the financial statements."

A few other key items from the exposure draft:

The financials are prepared from information provided by management.

Each page of the financial statements needs to include a comment there is no assurance on the financials provided by any CPA. Two example comments are:

> *No CPA provides any assurance on these financial statements.*

or

> *These financial statements have not been audited or reviewed, and no CPA expresses an opinion or a conclusion nor provides any assurance on them.*

If the accountant identifies any deficiencies or inaccuracies in the client provided information or there is obviously some missing info, the accountant needs to request management provide corrected or additional information. In other words, if something jumps out at the accountant, then the accountant needs to have management fix it.

Omitting substantially all disclosures is allowed.

The draft distinguishes between preparing financial statements and bookkeeping. These proposed rules apply to 'preparing' but not bookkeeping.

The difference is in the nature of services. Doing something like preparing bank reconciliations or depreciation schedules, drafting the notes, or proposing adjustments such as depreciation or deferred taxes would be 'preparing'. Merely doing the bookkeeping entries would not make the accountant's services subject to this exposure draft.

The proposed effective date is financial statements for years ending on or after 12-15-15. That translates to calendar year 2015 reports. Early implementation is allowed.

Football as illustration of differences between audits, reviews, and compilations

Since football season is in full swing, let's go to the nearest stadium to compare an audit to a review, to a compilation, and to the newest level of service, a preparation report.

Audit

If you were performing an audit, you would be on the field and receive the kickoff at your 20-yard line. A series of passes and runs would slowly move the ball. With effort you would advance to your opponent's 10-yard line. Good touchdown position.

Advancing the football would be the same as gathering evidence to provide you a reasonable level of assurance so you could issue an audit opinion on the financial statements.

That is the word picture provided by Mr. Mike Glynn, CPA, CGMA, Senior Technical Manager – AICPA Audit and Attest Standards Team, at the 2013 Accounting and Auditing Conference presented by the California Society of CPAs. With his knowledge, I'd like to share and expand his word picture. Any comments from him are his personal opinion. Any revisions to what he said or errors in this discussion are from me.

Review

So if you were providing a review at the football stadium, you would again receive the ball at your 20-yard line. After a series of advances by run and pass, you would get to the other side's 35-yard line. Out of touchdown range and at the edge of field goal range.

Those advances down the field would represent gathering evidence to provide you limited assurance to support your accountant's report.

Compilation

So if you were providing a compilation at the football stadium, you would again start at your 20-yard line, right?

Wrong.

You wouldn't be on the field.

You wouldn't even be inside the stadium.

You would be out in the parking lot eating a yummy burger with all the fixings fresh off the grill. You would not be advancing the ball down the field. Remember, you are outside the stadium.

You are neither advancing the ball in the football game nor gathering any evidence to provide assurance before you issue your compilation report.

Preparation report

The previous section introduced a new level of service that CPAs may be able to provide in the near future. It is called preparation of financial statements.

I want to extend the football illustration to this new service.

So if you were only preparing financial statements instead of providing a compilation at the football field would you be on the field?

No.

Would you be in the parking lot enjoying the grilled food at the tailgate party?

No.

You would be in your driveway putting beach chairs in the trunk of your car.

Not only are you not gathering evidence to support your report, you aren't anywhere near the football stadium. You are not a part of the event.

Sports wrapup

Audits and reviews are assurance engagements. They get you on the field advancing the ball. Or in professional terms, you are gathering assurance for your reporting.

So there you have it. Audits, reviews, compilations, and preparing a report are to CPA's work like advancing the football to the 10-yard line, only the 35-yard line, eating a burger in the parking lot, and going to the beach are to a football game.

How you would check out a used car if you audited, reviewed, or compiled its condition?

You could figure out how good a car is by looking at it from across the street.

Or you could look inside & drive it around the block.

Or you could take the car to your mechanic for a couple of hours to get it really checked out.

We can use that as an analogy of the differences between a compilation, a review, and an audit.

Stand across the street

You could try to figure out if that car would be a good one for you by looking at it from across the street. You could tell the make, model, and age give or take a year. You could see the body was intact and at least didn't have any crumpled bumpers. You can see that there are four tires on the ground but not their condition. You could see that all the windows are intact.

If you did that you could make a wild guess on the quality and price. But would you buy it based on that?

Not a chance.

That's sort of what a compilation is like. You've got an idea what the numbers are, but you really shouldn't make a 'buy' decision based on that.

Get inside and drive around the block

You could evaluate the quality of the car by getting inside, looking around, walking around the outside, looking under the hood, and taking a spin around the block.

What could you tell from that?

You would know the mileage, by looking at the plate on the door you could tell what month it was manufactured, and you could look around the interior to see what accessories it has and the condition of the upholstery. You could glance at the floorboard to see that the wear on the carpet is consistent with the mileage. You could look under the hood, listen to the engine for a minute and tell that it at least isn't a disaster. Drive around the block and you could tell that the transmission shifts smoothly, the car accelerates nicely, brakes smoothly without pulling. You could tell it has a decent muffler, air-conditioning, heating, and sound system.

Would you now have a better basis for estimating its price and quality? You bet.

Might you be willing to negotiate a purchase based on that? Lots and lots of people do.

That is sort of what a review is like. The CPA looks at the numbers, asks a few questions, looks at trends and relationships, ponders a minute, then decides there's nothing visibly wrong and issues a report.

Have a mechanic take it apart

You could take the car to a mechanic you trust. He would pull the tires, measure the tread, and inspect the brakes. He would look under the hood to see whether it has been steam cleaned recently. If yes, then something is being hidden, which is a warning sign something is wrong. If no, he could tell a lot. Maybe he can see that the alternator was replaced a few months ago and the water pump is only two or three years old. Maybe the radiator isn't OEM. That would suggest the previous owner took care of his vehicle. Maybe some parts are about to fall off.

A mechanic could look at the oil, tell you whether it was just changed, and if not whether there's metal in it. Maybe it's been years since it was changed. Likewise with the transmission fluid – is it brand-new fluid, way past when it should have been changed, or is there any metal in it? Inspecting the bottom of the engine tells you whether there are any new or recently repaired leaks. Hooking the engine up to the diagnostic equipment can give a really good understanding on the condition of the engine.

While you are waiting for your mechanic, you could check with DMV to see if there are any accident reports on the vehicle.

After he puts it all together you have a long heart-to-heart chat to find out the car's condition.

Do you now have a really good understanding of its condition? Yes. Do you have enough information to determine a very good price for the car? You bet. Can you make a really solid decision on whether you want the car or not and what a good price would be? Yeah.

That's sort of what an audit looks like. You have a lot more information on which to make a decision whether to buy or not.

Does that mean the transmission won't blow up next week or the air-conditioning won't fail the first week of summer? No. There's no guarantee.

But you have a lot better chance with a car the mechanic worked over than with something you drove around the block or something you just looked at from across the street.

How much will it cost to figure out the quality of that car?

What does it take in terms of time, money, and effort for each of those three options of figuring out the condition of the car?

Takes just a few moments and no cost to stand across the street and make a guess.

Takes some time and mental energy to look around the car and drive it around the block. You have to be thinking and observing very carefully.

Going to a mechanic will take you a few hours and cost you some money.

It comes down to a question of how much time, effort, and money you want to spend for the quality of information you get.

So here's my analogy:

Look at the car from across the street – very low cost for low quality information – **compilation.**

Look around inside in the car and drive it around the block - moderate cost for better information – **review.**

Have a mechanic work it over – highest cost in terms of time and money but the best information on the quality of the car – **audit.**

Audit. Review. Compilation.

A more detailed explanation of the differences

There are three different levels of services you could obtain from a certified public accountant. These are referred to as compilation, review, and audit.

Financial statements are presented on the basis of some set of accounting rules. This is referred to as the financial reporting framework.

The vast majority of the time, this would be a large body of knowledge that is called generally accepted accounting principles, or GAAP. Imperfect in implementation though it may be, the concept is that similar transactions will be recorded by all organizations in the same way. In addition, financial statements of similar organizations will actually look similar.

If there is some unique reason to do so, the financial statements could be presented on another basis of accounting.

<u>Compilation</u>

The goal of a compilation is to take information that is on the general ledger and accumulate it into financial statements in the same format that would come out of a review or audit. The format may look the same, but the accountant performs much less work in a compilation than in a review or audit.

The accountant will perform an extremely limited analysis on any of the numbers presented. The accountant would only follow up on information that is obviously incorrect, such as visible departures from the accounting rules. For example, if there are no depreciation expenses recorded when there should be, or if the amount of fixed assets is minimal even though there are substantial amounts of equipment in use, then the accountant would have to address the issue and make appropriate corrections.

There is an extreme limit on how much reliance can be placed on a compilation because the accountant has not gained an understanding of internal controls, has not even discussed with the organization how it is managing its fraud risks, and has not performed testing of any numbers.

One of the key sentences of a compilation report from the accountant reads:

> I have not audited or reviewed the accompanying financial statements and, accordingly, do not express an opinion or provide any assurance about whether the financial statements are in accordance with U.S. generally accepted accounting principles.

As a result, an external reader of the financial statements can place very minimal reliance on a compilation report.

A compilation is used when an outside party, such as a lender, needs to see the financial information in the format called for by the accounting rules instead of in whatever format the internal accounting system would produce. It is relatively rare for a small- or medium-sized nonprofit organization to obtain a compilation.

A compilation involves the lowest amount of work. As a result, the cost will be far lower than for a review or audit.

Review

The goal of a review is for the CPA to obtain limited assurance that the financial statements do not have any known errors or departures from the relevant accounting rules.

The procedures performed by the external accountant during a review will be limited to inquiries and analytical review. This means the accountant will ask many questions of management and the finance staff. If the answers to the questions suggest the accounting is appropriate, then no additional follow-up would be needed.

Analytical review means the accountant will look at the relationships between numbers to make sure they make sense. For example, if attendance at a local church is up about 10% from a year ago, then the amount of contributions from the congregation should have increased by something in the range of 10%. If contributions increased by much more or less than 10%, the accountant would ask management the reason for the unexpected change.

Another example is that if the full-time staff of an organization increased from twelve people to sixteen people, then wages, payroll taxes, and other benefits should have increased by something in the range of one-third. The accountant will follow-up with management on relationships in a financial statement that do not make sense based on an analytical review.

Normally, there will not be any testing of information in the financial statements beyond inquiry and analytical review. The accountant will not obtain an understanding of the internal control system and will not discuss how the organization is addressing the risk of fraud in the financial statements. As a result, there is a significant limit on how much reliance an external reader of the financial statements can place on the review report issued by the accountant.

One of the key sentences in a review report reads:

> Based on my reviews, I am not aware of any material modifications that should be made to the accompanying financial statements in order for them to be in conformity with U.S. generally accepted accounting principles.

A review is most often obtained when an outside party, such as a lender, needs to see the financial information in a typical format and is looking for some comfort level that the information can be relied upon.

The cost of a review is obviously more than a compilation and might be somewhere in the range of 40% to 60% of the cost of an audit.

Audit

The goal of an audit is for the CPA to obtain reasonable, but not absolute, assurance that the financial statements are fairly presented in accordance with the relevant accounting rules.

In an audit, the accountant will gain an understanding of internal controls, evaluate the risk of major fraud, test those places where there is a significant risk of major fraud, and perform testing as considered necessary for the significant components of the financial statements. A few examples of the type of testing involved would be confirming the amounts on deposit in banks, testing the cost of equipment, confirming with donors the amount of recorded contributions, and reviewing the supporting documentation for a number of disbursements.

There is a body of knowledge, called generally accepted auditing standards, that outlines the necessary work in an audit. The exact tests necessary are determined by the accountant based on his or her professional judgment.

An audit report provides a higher comfort level to a reader of the financial statements than a review or compilation. The CPA obtains for himself or herself a reasonable assurance that overall the financial statements are fairly presented in all material respects. This does not mean they are exactly correct. Since an audit could never test 100% of the transactions in an organization, there is a risk that untested transactions could be missing, mistaken, erroneous, or even fraudulent.

One of the key sentences in an audit report reads:

> In my opinion, the financial statements referred to above present fairly, in all material respects, the financial position of [nonprofit

name] as of December 31, [year], and the changes in its net assets and its cash flows for the year then ended in conformity with U.S. generally accepted accounting principles.

As a result, the external reader of the financial statements can be more comfortable that the financial statements are fairly presented.

An audit is most often obtained because a lender requires it as a condition of making a loan.

In the nonprofit community, there are many reasons to get an audit beyond the requirement of a lender. Going through the audit process communicates a higher level of accountability. Organizations that give money to nonprofits often require an audit as a condition of making a grant. Federal funding over a certain threshold creates a requirement to go through the audit process.

Many nonprofit organizations voluntarily go through an audit because it subjects them to scrutiny by an outsider.

Also, some voluntary membership organizations, such as the Evangelical Council for Financial Accountability, require an audit as a condition of membership. The ECFA requires members with income over $3,000,000 per year to submit audited financial statements. Below $1,500,000 of revenue, their members may submit compiled financial statements. In between those two amounts, reviewed financial statements are necessary.

The cost of an audit will be substantially higher than a review or compilation.

Filling up a bucket with water – word picture for levels of assurance in audit, review, and compilation

In a webcast back in 2011, Mike Glynn, CPA, CGMA, gave a wonderful word picture of the levels of assurance in a review and audit. As I mentioned earlier, Mr. Glynn is Senior Technical Manager – AICPA Audit and Attest Standards Team.

Here's the idea: Filling up a bucket with procedures produces different levels of assurance. Here is my expanded description of that idea.

In an audit, the accountant obtains reasonable assurance that there are no material errors in the financial statements.

In a review, the accountant obtains limited assurance that there are no material errors in the financial statements.

In a compilation, the accountant does not obtain any assurance that there are no material errors in the financial statements.

Notice the similarity and difference? The overlap between these definitions is how much assurance the accountant obtains for himself or herself that there are no material errors in the financial statements.

The differences?

In a compilation? No assurance.

In a review? Limited assurance.

In an audit? Reasonable assurance– which is a high level

The visual illustration is filling up a bucket. The bucket is the amount of assurance. You pour water into the bucket and check to see how full it is. Pour in just a few procedures and inquiries, check the bucket, and realize it's not very full. Add a few more procedures and inquiries and analytical procedures, check the bucket, and realize you're up to the level of limited assurance.

The bucket is somewhere in the range of one-third or half full. You're ready to issue a review report.

Pour in a bunch more water with the idea of getting the bucket almost full. Pour in a lot of inquiries, a bunch of predictive tests, and confirmations in some areas. Go look at the inventory, talk to management and employees about fraud, and pour in a bunch of discussions of internal control, then check the bucket. You see that it is pretty full and realize you have reached the 'reasonable' level of assurance.

Imagine a bucket that has water to within maybe an inch or so from the top.

You're ready to issue an audit opinion.

What about a compilation?

In spite of the wording of a compilation report, my opinion is that the level of assurance is not actually at zero. There is a very low level of assurance for the accountant that is built into the financial statements that go along with a compilation report. It is really low, but there is still some water in the bucket.

For example, the accountant knows that the numbers actually tie back to the client's general ledger. Income accounts are in the revenue part of the income statement and expense accounts are shown as an expense. If the accountant sees property and equipment, there should be some sort of depreciation recorded. If an organization extends credit to customers, the accountant checks to see there are receivables recorded and an allowance for uncollectible accounts.

What is the conceptual support for this? If there are really obvious errors in compiled financial statements, the accountant has to address them.

Two illustrations just mentioned are depreciation expense and an allowance for doubtful accounts. A company that has lots of property and equipment that is used in running the business should have depreciation. If the depreciation expense account is zero, the accountant cannot just ignore that in a compilation. If the company is extending credit to all customers and it usually takes customers a few weeks to pay, then there will be a bunch of receivables. If the receivable balance is zero, the number is obviously wrong. In this miserable economy, it would be really weird for the allowance for doubtful accounts at that client to be zero. Even in a compilation, an accountant should ask about an allowance that is zero.

The end result is that the numbers in a compilation report could be way off — so far off that the errors would change the decisions of anyone reading the financial statements. By the way that's the definition of material. However, the really, really obvious stuff would be fixed. I suggest that "no assurance" is not zero assurance.

Picture a bucket that only has an inch or two of water in the bottom. There's not much water, but there is some.

The level of water needed is a matter of professional judgment. You may reach a considered opinion that this much water gives you limited assurance. I might conclude I need more water to be at the limited assurance level. My buddy at another CPA firm might conclude that the cutoff for limited assurance is lower than what you and I believe. That is what professional judgment is all about.

I don't know how to quantify the levels of assurance. But these imaginary buckets give a vague relationship.

Audit. Review. Compilation.

More discussion on levels of assurance gained by the CPA

I'll try to give a little more detail on what those different levels of assurance look like.

Picture the comfort level, or assurance, as a continuum with zero, or no assurance at one end. At the other end, there is 100% assurance, or a guarantee that the numbers are exactly, precisely, perfectly correct. Where then would a review, audit and compilation show up on that continuum?

When CPAs issue a compilation report on financial statements, the report says "We have not audited or reviewed the accompanying financial statements and, accordingly, do not express an opinion or any other form of assurance" on them. What this is telling the reader is that the numbers are all from management, so don't look to us CPAs for any comfort that the numbers, classifications, and disclosures are right.

At the other end of the spectrum, when a CPA issues an audit report on the financial statements, this means the accountant has gained reasonable, but not absolute, assurance for himself or herself that financial statements are fairly presented in accordance with the accounting rules. Reasonable assurance is a fairly high level of assurance. This means you can know that the accountant has a reasonable comfort level that the amounts, classifications, presentation, and disclosures are all in sync with the relevant accounting rules.

In between is a review. A review means the accountant has obtained for him or herself limited assurance that financial statements do not have any known errors or departures from the accounting rules. This means if the CPA identified any errors, mistakes or omissions, they were fixed. Doesn't mean there won't be huge errors in the numbers. It means that just based on looking at the relationships between the numbers and asking management a few questions, the CPA didn't notice anything obvious.

The previous section tries to translate these relationships into a visual picture. Three things to point out.

First, "no assurance" on a compilation does not mean "zero". The irony is the accountant gained some small amount of assurance. Why? Because if there is something really, really out-of-line, the CPA is obligated to discuss it with management and see that it is fixed. An example would be if the general ledger shows a lot of property and equipment but there is no depreciation expense. Or one of the big expenses is called loan payments but the balance sheet does not show any change in the loan balances, which means the loan was not amortized. In those cases, the CPA would track down the odd issue and make sure the financials get fixed. In one case depreciation needs to be recorded and in the other case some of the loan payment need to be applied to the loan balance. In addition, the CPA would read through the disclosures to make sure they contain all the items that should be present. In this example, there would be fixed asset and long term debt disclosures that must be made. If they are missing, the CPA would ask management to change the notes.

So, you can see the accountant obtained some low, minimal level of comfort about the financial statements. Again, why? Because the CPA would read the financial statements and make sure the really big stuff was at least included. It might be off by a lot, but at least the disclosures are included. "No assurance" isn't the same as zero assurance.

Second, an audit is a long way from 100% assurance. It is impossible to make sure that financial statements are 100% right. Thus an auditor cannot gain 100% comfort on them.

Why? Many reasons. One hundred percent assurance would cost a fortune and take 3 or 6 months to perform the work. Sometimes the assumptions and estimates needed to develop financial statements are so difficult to determine that it might take years to find out if all of those assumptions and estimates are exactly correct. Finally there is human error. It is not possible to be 100% sure that there wasn't some mistake made by staff, honest error by management, something missed by the auditor, or something missed by everyone. There are still more reasons, but you get the point. In my opinion, an audit is further away from 100% comfort level than a compilation is away from zero.

Third, a review gives the accountant some assurance but not a high amount. A review is in between but closer to a compilation than an audit. I cannot quantify each of the above points, but I would perceive that a review is below the half way point, probably by quite a bit.

There is my description of the relationships between a compilation, a review, and an audit, along with my interpretation of why they land on the continuum of assurance at different points.

About the Author

James L. Ulvog has over 25 years experience as a CPA. Since 1989, he has focused on working in the religious nonprofit environment providing audits, reviews, and consulting services. Since 2002, he has run his own accounting firm in Alta Loma, California, and is intentionally a one-person office. Most of his experience is working with small- to medium-sized organizations.

Mr. Ulvog is blogging at several sites on different topics. You can visit his weblogs at:

Nonprofit Update (nonprofitupdate.**info**) - addressing issues of interest to the nonprofit community

Outrun Change (outrunchange.com) - trying to cope with the overwhelming change surrounding all of us

Attestation Update (attestationupdate.com) - issues of interest to CPAs and accountants

Prior to starting his own firm, Mr. Ulvog worked for a national CPA firm known for its focus on the nonprofit community. His earliest CPA experience was with two international firms. He currently leads an adult Bible study. He currently serves as an elder at his church. He served on the board of a local nonprofit organization for 11 years.

Other books by this author

Step Up to the Next Level: A Guide for Local Churches to Improve Their Internal Operations and Prepare for an Audit

Written specifically for local churches, this primer will help you step up to the basic level of internal controls and procedures every church should have. It describes key information on the audit process to help your church step up to the level of getting a financial review or audit.

Key topics:

- Why bother putting good procedures in place? (Hint: the rules have changed.)
- Fundamental financial procedures.
- How internal controls protect your staff.
- Basic internal controls that can be easily developed.
- Overview of what the audit process looks like, including recent changes you will hear about as you move into an audit.

Whatever controls your church has in place, this guide will help you step up to the next level of accountability.

Once Upon Internal Control - A tale of good and bad ways to implement internal controls in a local church

This is a fable of two churches

...One Church ignores internal procedures and pays a steep price

...Another implements good procedures and can focus on mission

This fable of two churches shows how the quality of internal controls can either prevent bad things from happening, as is the case in Southside Community Church, or allow them to take place undetected, which is the sad story at Northside. Lessons learned from each church are discussed after the story of their experiences. This short book illustrates some very simple and basic procedures you can put in place in any local church. Many small churches need to implement the controls illustrated here.

The more internal controls you can put in place, the more protection you will provide for your church, your pastor, and your staff. If you are in any position of responsibility in the financial area, these controls can help protect you.

This fable is only 9 pages long, so it is a very quick read. It would be a good introduction to internal control for your board or pastoral staff.

The ideas described would also apply to other nonprofit organizations.

Tragedy of Fraud - The Ripple Effects from Fraud and the Wages Earned

There are tragic consequences from fraud that spread out to harm innocent bystanders. The perpetrator draws a wide range of well-deserved wages that will be paid in full.

The book looks at two fraud incidents to learn what happens after a fraud is discovered. One took place in a local megachurch and the other in the mayor's office of a small city.

This book is a compilation of previously published blogs posts.

Major sections of the book:

- Tragedy of Fraud – The ripple effects from the embezzlement fraud in a local church.
- Wages of Fraud – Consequences from the corruption fraud in a mayor's office.
- Why is it Difficult to Find Fraud? – The lack of documentation inside an organization makes it even more difficult to identify a fraud scheme.
- The Fraud Triangle – A discussion of the three sides of a fraud triangle. That's the idea that three components need to be present for a fraud to take place – opportunity, motivation, and rationalization. Great danger is in play when all three factors are present.

For more information on these and other books, along with information on where to find them, visit the website of the publisher of this book: *Riverstone Finance Press* at riverstonefinancepress.com.

www.ingramcontent.com/pod-product-compliance
Lightning Source LLC
Chambersburg PA
CBHW060500200326
41520CB00017B/4869